JARROLD SHORT WALKS
leisure walks for all ages

Around Cardiff

Compiled by
Terry Marsh

JARROLD
publishing

 Mapping sourced from

 Ordnance Survey®

Text: Terry Marsh
Photography: Terry Marsh
Editor: Crawford Gillan
Designer: Sarah Crouch

Jarrold Publishing ISBN 0-7117-3005-9

While every care has been taken to
ensure the accuracy of the route
directions, the publishers cannot
accept responsibility for errors or
omissions, or for changes in details
given. The countryside is not static:
hedges and fences can be removed,
field boundaries can be altered,
footpaths can be rerouted and
changes in ownership can result in the
closure or diversion of some
concessionary paths. Also, paths that
are easy and pleasant for walking in
fine conditions may become slippery,
muddy and difficult in wet weather,
while stepping-stones across rivers
and streams may become impassable.

If you find an inaccuracy in either the
text or maps, please write or e-mail to
Jarrold Publishing at the addresses
below.

First published 2004
by Jarrold Publishing

Printed in Belgium
by Proost NV, Turnhout. 1/04

Jarrold Publishing
Pathfinder Guides, Whitefriars,
Norwich NR3 1JR
E-mail: info@totalwalking.co.uk
www.totalwalking.co.uk

Front cover: Miniature railway, Margam
Country Park
Previous page: On Mynydd Maen
Common

Contents

Keymap

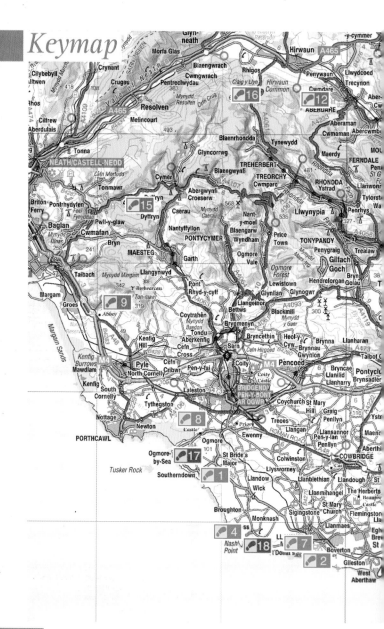

SCALE 1:384 615 or 1 INCH to about 6 MILES *1CM to 3.8KM*

0 2 4 6 8 10 KILOMETRES 15

0   2   4   6 MILES 8   10

KEYMAP HEIGHTS SHOWN IN FEET

Introduction

The routes and information in this book have been devised specifically with families and children in mind. All the walks include points of interest as well as a question to provide an objective.

If you, or your children, have not walked before, choose from the shorter walks for your first outings, although none of the walks is especially demanding. The purpose is not simply to get from A to B, but to enjoy an exploration, which may be just a steady stroll in the countryside, alongside rivers and lakes, or through woodlands.

The walks are graded by length and difficulty, but few landscapes are truly flat, so even short walks may involve some ascent, although this is nowhere excessive. Details are given under 'Route Features' in the first information box for each walk. The precise nature of the ground underfoot, however, will depend on recent weather conditions. If you do set out on a walk and discover the going is harder than you expected, or

Coastal Cliffs at Dunraven Bay

Mynydd Maen Common

the weather has deteriorated, do not be afraid to turn back. The route will always be there another day, when you are fitter or the children are more experienced or the weather is better. Few of the walks in this book involve rough terrain (although there are a number of steep climbs and some muddy going after rain), but it is always advisable to wear proper walking footwear rather than trainers or wellington boots.

Bear in mind that the countryside is constantly changing. Landmarks may disappear, gates may becomes stiles, rights-of-way may be altered, permissive paths may close. In quite a few places the terrain can be confusing, and this means having to pay rather close attention to route descriptions and waymarking or, in the absence of waymarking, the general direction followed by the path. But none of the walks is so complex as to deter anyone.

Some of the paths are seasonally overgrown. This presents two problems: one is difficulty in following the route underfoot; the other is the soaking you may get from overgrowth if you do the walk after rain, or stinging by nettles, which will be a problem for young children and also makes the wearing of shorts something to be wary of. Arable fields, while invariably having a wide field header to walk along, often have crops that spread or

Lighthouse, Nash Point

are blown down by the wind, and this obscures the 'kerb' between the field margin and the crop, producing the risk of ankle sprain. Occasionally you will find footpaths that have been cropped over or ploughed; this is usually a temporary thing, and the footpath is generally back in place before long.

Cardiff and its environs

Only one of the walks in this book is actually in Cardiff; all the others plunder the lovely countryside that surrounds it. The coastline, too, is a delight to walk, so the author makes no apology for making the most of it.

What is really surprising – some might say – is the quality of the countryside visited in this book. This is an area, remember, that was heavily ingrained in coal-mining and other dirty and heavy industries. But today all that has gone and in its place the reclamation has been astounding. If you come to South Wales and the valleys expecting grime and squalor, think again – you are in for a surprise, and an agreeable one at that.

Along the coast there are some truly splendid walks, whether from Ogmore-by-Sea or Nash Point, and just inland, the lovely villages of Llantwit Major and St Donat's. Elsewhere, the walks explore a number of country and forest parks – one, Margam, based around a mock-Tudor mansion with herds of deer in the grounds. Virtually all the country parks are developed on reclaimed land, although you can hardly tell. And the forests have now matured and provide a cloak to mask the remnants of industry until, finally, Nature takes it all back.

Red deer, Margam Country Park

The flora and fauna are excellent. Some of the country parks have rare species like marsh fritillary butterfly, crossbills and goshawks, while the coastal cliffs are host to peregrine falcon, kestrel, fulmars and butterflies like clouded yellow, silver-washed fritillary, common blue, argus and ringlets. It is quite remarkable and makes carrying binoculars, and even identification books, well worthwhile. And don't overlook the wild flowers either. Many of the woodlands are a joy in spring and early summer when the bluebells are rampant. But at other times you will find a great range that includes germander speedwell, toadflax and scarlet pimpernel. And, if you come at the right time of year, you can stock up on elderberries, blackberries, bilberries, and sloes – to flavour your gin.

Afan Country Park

Cosmeston Lakes

For me, pride of place (away from the coasts) goes to Parc Cwm Darran above the lovely village of Deri, north of Ystrad Mynach. This really was a heavily industrialised spot, sited where the Ogilvie Colliery once stood. But to look at it now, all you see are smooth, rounded hillsides, mature woodlands, reed-fringed lakes and clear, refreshing air. The transformation is spectacular. And while Parc Cwm Darran is to be especially commended, other parks trail not far behind, making this part of Wales a place of outstanding landscape and cultural heritage.

The peak-baggers will find among these walks, three 'Marilyns' – hills with at least 500 ft (150m) of re-ascent. And although some walks do visit 'summits', none of the routes is unduly demanding – Cwm Carn being the most severe. Elsewhere, you can begin your conquest of Britain's mountains with comparative ease – or you can just relax by a crystal stream and take in the beauty that surrounds Cardiff.

1 *Dunraven Bay*

START Near Southerndown
DISTANCE 2 miles (3.2km)
TIME 1 hour
PARKING Car parks on road down to Dunraven Bay (charge)
ROUTE FEATURES Woodland trails; farmland; coastal path

This very short walk combines the secluded loveliness of Dunraven Bay with a wander across the adjacent coastal lands, visiting one of only a few pubs in this area, and one that caters well for children.

Start from the beach car park (although the higher one will serve just as well, and is less likely to be full – the charge is the same), and bear left along a lane leading to the heritage centre. Have a look at the lovely thatchwork on the cottage opposite the heritage centre: thatch is quite common in this part of Wales, but absent from a large section of Britain.

Go past the cottage and bear left to a gate giving into Slade Wood. The path, still surfaced, continues through the wood and, at the far end, bears right to a gate giving into the corner of a sloping field. Beyond the gate, keep left along the field boundary (no discernible path).

Dunraven Bay

PUBLIC TRANSPORT Buses to Southerndown
REFRESHMENTS Pub in Southerndown
PUBLIC TOILETS At start
ORDNANCE SURVEY MAPS Landranger 170 (Vale of Glamorgan), Explorer 151 (Cardiff & Bridgend)

Trees that grow close to windswept coastlines are often blown into weird shapes. See if you can find any.

Towards the far side of the field, bear away from the woodland on the left to aim for a flight of concrete steps **A** that lead up to a stone stile. In the next two fields, keep to the left-hand boundary, following a wall.

Finally, a stone stile gives onto the Southerndown road. Turn left and walk down the road to pass the

Three Golden Cups pub. Just past the pub, leave the main road by branching left onto a side road for the beach, but immediately bear right at the telephone box.

Pebble beach, Dunraven Bay

Walk along a short road as far as a metal kissing-gate on the right (footpath signpost). Go across the centre of the ensuing meadow aiming for the end of a collapsed wall (waymark). From this, keep on in the same direction, to locate a stone stile in the corner of the next field. Over this, bear right, following a wall to a stile giving onto a road. Turn left, and, *taking care against approaching traffic*, walk down the road, crossing a cattle-grid **B**.

A little farther on, turn left with the wall as it runs along the coastline. Stay parallel with the wall, keeping well above the cliffs, and later moving towards a fenceline on the left. Pass through a gate to access the higher (Cymla) car park. Leave the car park by a wall gap near the pay machine, and beyond walk down a grassy path beside the road all the way back to Dunraven Bay. ●

Walks such as those in this book are ideal for beginning a lifelong fascination with **wild flowers**. Most people will be satisfied with simply finding and naming flowers, but for some the pursuit becomes a delightful hobby.

Llantwit Coast

START Llantwit Major beach
DISTANCE 2 miles (3.2km)
TIME 1 hour
PARKING Llantwit Major beach
ROUTE FEATURES Clifftop paths; farm fields; country lanes

2

This is an outstandingly easy walk, but it is sheer delight on a warm summer's day. The views are excellent, and the range of butterflies to be found throughout the walk is certain to delay progress as you try to identify them all.

Begin from the entrance to the car park by climbing wooden steps to gain a zigzagging path that leads up onto the headland, and there bear left alongside a fence to reach the clifftop.

Go through a kissing-gate, and a short way on encounter the earthwork known as Castle Ditches, now shrouded in scrubby woodland. This is the site of an Iron Age hillfort.

Beyond, press on along the edge of an arable field, with the clifftop on the right. This lofty section is a delight to follow, but eventually the path starts to descend as it approaches Pigeon Point **A**.

Here, just on reaching a stile, turn left (don't cross the stile), and walk alongside a fence and hedgerow, heading inland. As the path approaches Rosedew Farm, it feeds into a wide, hedged track that leads to the farm. Keep to the right of the farm buildings, to gain a lane leading out to a road **B**.

Glamorgan coastline

PUBLIC TRANSPORT Buses to Llantwit Major
REFRESHMENTS At the beach
PUBLIC TOILETS At start
ORDNANCE SURVEY MAPS Landranger 170 (Vale of Glamorgan), Explorer 151 (Cardiff & Bridgend)

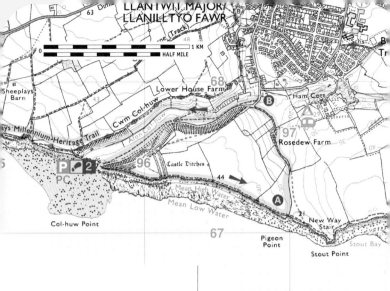

At the road, turn right for 35 yds (30m), as far as a metal kissing-gate on the left, and here leave the road. Beyond the gate, a clear path crosses rough pasture. Continue

Along the Llantwit coast

? *This walk is ideal for spotting butterflies that love the vegetation, especially along the clifftops. See how many different species you can find.*

through another kissing-gate and then on once more along a clear path heading back towards the beach, passing down the length of Cwm Col-huw. ●

There are 62 species of **butterfly** in Britain, 54 of them are 'resident' and breed here, plus eight that are migrants. Many butterflies have declined in numbers, mainly because of subtle climate changes and modern farming practices.

Castell Coch and Fforest Fawr

3

START Castell Coch
DISTANCE 2¼ miles (3.6km)
TIME 1 hour
PARKING Castell Coch
ROUTE FEATURES Woodland trails

Castell Coch is an amazing building, its round and pointed turrets rising dramatically from the enclosing woodland like medieval space rockets, although in reality they are no older than the 19th century. The woodlands that back the castle have numerous routes through them, many of them waymarked, and all open for exploration; this walk samples a couple, in a generally easy circuit.

Castell Coch was built for the **Marquess of Bute**, on the site of a ruined medieval castle. It was a Victorian endeavour to fulfil a rich man's dream to recreate a 13th-century Welsh castle, complete with drawbridge and portcullis. The interior of the castle is extravagantly decorated and quite stunning.

Set off from the car park for the disabled near the castle by heading onto the signposted Woodland Trail, which immediately starts to climb. The ascent ends when the path meets the Taff Trail at a waymark **A**.

Here keep forward (bearing right) along a broad woodland track, flanked in spring and summer with flowers that are especially attractive to butterflies. On my last visit, one large buddleia (among many) had no fewer than eight species of butterfly on it at the same time – small tortoiseshell, painted lady, brimstone, peacock, red admiral, speckled wood, small white and silver-washed fritillary. It is always worth carrying an identification book, or at least a notebook, to jot down the points of identification.

PUBLIC TRANSPORT Buses along Taff Vale
REFRESHMENTS Teashop in castle grounds
PUBLIC TOILETS Inside castle
ORDNANCE SURVEY MAPS Landranger 171 (Cardiff & Newport); Explorer 151 (Cardiff & Bridgend)

Castell Coch

Continue along the woodland trail, which maintains much the same direction, and eventually runs out of the woodland just beyond a car park. But, about 220 yds (200m) before reaching the car park, leave the broad trail by doubling back to the right onto a narrow path entering the woodland shade **B**.

The path descends gently through stands of beech and scattered pine, and runs on to intercept another at a T-junction **C**. Turn left, descending, and, at the next path junction, turn right along a route waymarked with blue-topped poles. Keep following the blue trail, which later swings left to intercept a horizontal track. Now, turn left, leaving the blue trail, and following a descending path, passing a number of joining paths.

The path finally emerges from the woodland at the foot of the driveway up to Castell Coch. Turn right to return to the start. ●

? *See if you can find a huge wooden arch.*

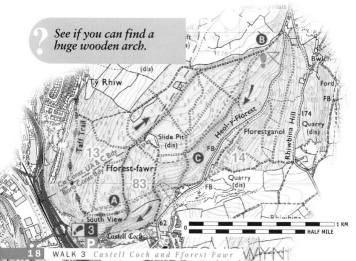

The Heritage Coast

START Nash Point, Marcross
DISTANCE 2½ miles (4km)
TIME 1 hour
PARKING Nash Point (Charge)
ROUTE FEATURES Sea cliff and farmland paths

4

This linear walk (out and back) is an unashamed excuse to get the most from the stunning coastline overlooking the Bristol Channel. The walk simply goes as far as Cwm Nash, and then comes back by exactly the same route. It is possible to double the length of the walk by going up through Cwm Nash for a pub lunch in Monknash, or you can take a picnic and enjoy it at the foot of Cwm Nash.

The route directions could not be easier. From the refreshment kiosk turn right and descend into Cwm Marcross, heading up an obvious grassy gully **A** on the other side to climb up to a stile giving into a large arable field.

The promontory here is worth a visit (*but do keep children away from the edges as there is no clifftop protection*). There used to be an Iron Age hill-fort here, one of a number along the Glamorgan coastline. These were built between about 700 BC and the arrival of the Roman forces in the first century AD. The inhabitants were probably farmers.

The cliffs at Nash Point are made up of a series of limestone rock layers, separated by soft layers of shale. The shale weathers more quickly, removing the support for the limestone, which ultimately collapses into the sea. *Bear in mind that a collapse could happen at any time; so stay well clear.*

See if you can spot any fulmars.

PUBLIC TRANSPORT Buses to Marcross
REFRESHMENTS Kiosk at Nash Point, pubs in Marcross and Monknash
PUBLIC TOILETS None on route
ORDNANCE SURVEY MAPS Landranger 170 (Vale of Glamorgan), Explorer 151 (Cardiff & Bridgend)

Along the Heritage Coast

Bear left along the edge of the arable field, and, at the far side, cross another stile and then simply maintain the same direction across a number of fields, with ever-changing views of the coastline.

Keep an eye open, too, for peregrine falcons, ravens, kestrels and a host of coastal birds. Many butterflies also favour this breezy habitat, including clouded yellow, speckled wood, common blue,

painted lady and red admiral.

At Cwm Nash **B**, a clear path zigzags down to the foot of the wooded cwm, and from this point simply return by the outward route.

One of the joys of **birdwatching** is that of discovery – the more unusual, the better. The walks in this book are perfect for getting to know a good range of species.

Nash Point Cliffs

5 *Porthkerry Park*

START Porthkerry, Barry
DISTANCE 2½ miles
(4.2km)
TIME 1 hour
PARKING Car park at start
ROUTE FEATURES
Woodland trails;
farmland

Porthkerry is a delightful wooded country park on the outskirts of Barry. There are historical links with the old village of Cwmcidi to the north of the park, and a close encounter with a spectacular viaduct. But generally this simple walk is about wandering across lovely landscapes.

From the parking area, set off on the paved path passing the pitch-and-putt course. Walk down towards the pebble beach but, before reaching it, turn left and soon cross a metal footbridge, swinging left to the foot of steps. Here turn right, up the steps.

Keep forward from the top of the steps along a surfaced path that skirts through the edge of woodland comprising ash, beech, hazel, hawthorn, sycamore, holly and oak. When the path forks, branch left, and follow a line of old fenceposts.

> **?** *How many steps are there beside the handrail climbing out of the park near the start of the walk?*

The path presses on to run behind residential properties, and finally emerges onto a pavement area in front of apartments. Keep forward to a T-junction **A**, and there turn left, walking down beside the access road into the park.

In 1944 military vehicles gathered in the park before embarkation for France, when 21 ships left Barry Docks for the Normandy landings.

PUBLIC TRANSPORT Buses to Porthkerry
REFRESHMENTS Café in country park
PUBLIC TOILETS At start
ORDNANCE SURVEY MAPS Landranger 170 (Vale of Glamorgan) and 171 (Cardiff & Newport), Explorer 151 (Cardiff & Bridgend)

Continue down the lane as far as a signposted footpath on the right, and here go down steps into the woodland, and then cross a footbridge. Over the bridge, bear left along a path, into the park.

Keep forward to walk alongside the main driveway. Cross another footbridge and a small car park, and then walk towards a single arch railway viaduct **B**. Turn right just before the viaduct, keeping to the right of a gate and fence onto a narrow, ascending path into light woodland.

Eventually, the path moves away from the nearby railway line and climbs farther into the woodland, to a stile at the top edge of the woodland. Turn left, and head for

a powerline pole across the field, near West Ridge Farm, and locate a step-stile in the field corner. Cross another stile a short way farther on, now with Cardiff Airport in view.

Porthkerry farmland

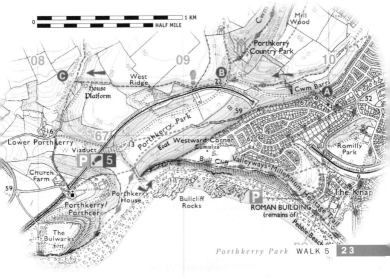

From the stile, aim across the centre of the ensuing field to a metal gate where a step-stile gives into the next field. Turn immediately right along the field boundary to another stile 45 yds (40m) away. The edges of these farmland pastures are a good place to keep an eye open for wild flowers that enjoy undisturbed land, like scarlet pimpernel and germander speedwell, both of which can be found at this point.

Over the stile, and bear left down the field edge to the bottom of the field and there bear left and then right around a ruined cottage to go down towards Whitelands Brook ❸. Cross the brook by a footbridge followed by a stile, and over this turn left along the bottom edge of a field to a pair of stiles

nearby. Over these, go forward along a bramble hedgerow until, at a gap, you can pass through to the opposite side, and then keep on to the bottom left-hand corner of the field.

Cross a stile giving onto an old sunken track and path, which leads out to a narrow lane. Turn left and follow a stony track towards the railway viaduct. Walk under the viaduct and bear left to complete the walk. ●

> The **viaduct** was built in the 19th century and has 13 arched spans. The line opened in 1897 but was instantly followed by a disaster when one of the piers slipped. The line reopened two years later and is still in use today. It carries coal to **Aberthaw** power station.

The viaduct

Cosmeston Lakes

START Cosmeston
DISTANCE 3 miles (5km)
TIME 1½ hours
PARKING Cosmeston
Lakes Country Park
ROUTE FEATURES
Woodland trails;
lakeside paths

Cosmeston Lakes are the by-product of quarrying, and today provide an ideal habitat for birds, butterflies and flora. An adventure play area, easy walks and a chance to feed the ducks makes this an immensely popular place with children. Nearby, a 14th-century village has been recreated to give an insight into life in medieval times. The walk is very easy, but a visit to the country park is certain to make it longer.

Start from the car park and walk to the eastern lake, turning right onto a broad, surfaced path, and follow this around the edge of the lake.

When the hedgerow on the right – which contains a range of bushes including the blackthorn with seasonal crops of sloes – comes to an end, leave the main track by branching right to gain a broad track.

Follow this beyond a gate, and keep an eye open for green woodpeckers which populate the woodland on your right and can often be seen flying away ahead of you – just one of 112 species that favour this area.

When the on-going track forks, branch right, now onto a narrower

A good range of **butterflies** also find the hedgerows here, which in spring are bright with a lovely display of wild flowers, very much to their liking. Keep an eye open for clouded yellow, painted lady, large and small skipper, holly blue, red admiral, peacock and many more.

PUBLIC TRANSPORT Buses to Cosmeston
REFRESHMENTS Café at visitor centre
PUBLIC TOILETS At start
ORDNANCE SURVEY MAPS Landranger 171 (Cardiff & Newport), Explorer 151 (Cardiff & Bridgend)

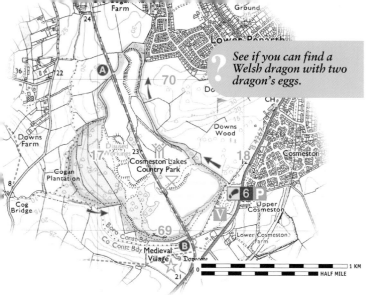

path. Eventually, this leads round to another set of gates giving onto the main access track that runs through the centre of the country park **A**. Cross this, and continue in the same direction on the other side, through another gate.

At the next set of gates, remain on the main path, now broader and bearing right. The pathways here are a delight to wander, and worth lingering over. While doing so, cast an eye over adjoining fields on the off-chance of spotting buzzards or kestrels. As the track reaches a T-junction, near a waymark (M10), turn right, and when it next meets a main junction **B**, go forward onto a path opposite (waymark Q12).

The ongoing path immediately forks. Branch left and walk through woodland cover to another junction not far from a lake edge. Turn right, and soon reach a boardwalk, with, a short way on, a helpful interpretive lay-by. Follow the boardwalk back to the visitor centre.

Cosmeston Lakes

Llantwit Major

START Llantwit Major beach
DISTANCE 3 miles (5km)
TIME 2 hours
PARKING Car park at the beach
ROUTE FEATURES Woodland trails; country lanes; coastal path

Cross the beach car park and go to the left of the café and then turn around the back of it onto a concrete path leading to the foot of steps. Turn up these and, at the top, bear right at a bench and walk along a clear path to a stile. Continue along the path beyond, which passes between established hedgerows.

🖌 Among the hedgerows, keep a lookout for sloes (the fruit of the blackthorn), elderberries and brambles.

The path soon levels and leads on above Cwm Col-huw. Beyond a second stile, the path gives onto a stony track. Just as this starts to descend towards Lower House Farm leave it by branching left to a metal kissing-gate **Ⓐ**. From this, head up the middle of the next field on an indistinct grassy path. Continue across the field and go through a hedge gap on the far right-hand side, and then go immediately left to a gate and stile.

Over the stile, bear right along a field boundary and, on the far side, gain a sunken track (Church Lane). Turn right and, when the lane bends to the left, leave it and go forward to cross a stone stile. In the ensuing field, head diagonally left, aiming for the village church and the round tower of a medieval dovecote; there is no path along this section. Keep to the right of the dovecote to locate another stone stile in front of a row of white cottages.

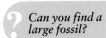

? *Can you find a large fossil?*

PUBLIC TRANSPORT Buses to Llantwit Major
REFRESHEMNTS Café at the beach; pubs and café in Llantwit Major
PUBLIC TOILETS At start
ORDNANCE SURVEY MAPS Landranger 170 (Vale of Glamorgan), Explorer 151 (Cardiff & Bridgend)

Turn left, and continue forward into the village to visit the church, which is dedicated to St Illtud, one of the Celtic saints who spread Christianity throughout Wales, Ireland and Cornwall after the departure of the Romans.

At Llantwit Major, St Illtud established a church and monastery which became an important centre of missionary activity from which people went out to preach the Gospel. The church is, in fact, two churches stuck together. The oldest part is the western end, which probably stands on the site of **St Illtud's** 6th-century church, and was built by the Normans around 1100. The east church was built in the 13th century and then, in the 15th century, the west church was rebuilt. As a result, the oldest part of the entire building has the newest features. The church is quite outstanding, not only as a centre for Christian worship, but architecturally, too. Its **wall paintings**, while not unique, are remarkable and its 'collection' of effigies and crosses will require time to take it all in. In the churchyard is a medieval preaching cross. The head had been destroyed, but it was restored in 1919 and set up again on the original base.

On leaving the church, walk back up towards the row of white cottages, but just before them, turn right at the Gatehouse, into a side lane **B**. On the hill overlooking the church, there used to be a group of monastic buildings, entered through the gatehouse, a 13th-century building.

Follow the lane beyond the Old Vicarage, continuing ahead onto a path between hedgerows. A short way on, as the hedged path swings left, leave it by going forward over a stile. Go along the left-hand edge of the ensuing field. On the far side another stone stile awaits, and beyond this again keep to the left-hand edge of a pasture. This leads up to a step-stile and gate, from which cross to the far right-hand corner of the next field. Then maintain the same direction across two fields, one small, the second rather larger, followed by a narrow enclosure after which you enter a large arable field.

Dovecote

Head straight across the field, aiming for the right-hand edge of a stand of trees in the distance. At the far edge of the woodland, pass into the adjacent field, and resume the same direction aiming now for the ruins of Sheeplays Barn ahead.

C Cross another stile and keep forward to the barn (signposted to Tresilian). Pass to the right of the barn, and simply keep going to reach the upper edge of Cwm Tresilian **D**. Here, cross a stile and go down steps, then alongside a woodland boundary on a clear path that leads out to meet the coastal path at a stile.

Turn left, soon passing a pillbox from World War II **E**, and follow the coastal path all the way back to Llantwit beach to complete the walk.

Preaching Cross

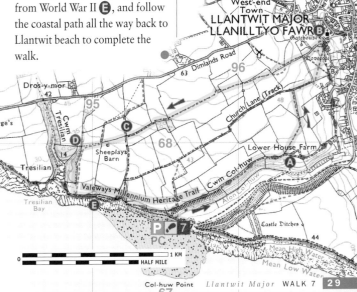

8 *Merthyr Mawr*

START Candleston
DISTANCE 3 miles (5km)
TIME 2 hours
PARKING At start (charge)
ROUTE FEATURES Sandy woodland trails; farm fields; country lanes; road walking

The sand dunes that make up Twmpath Mawr are only a short distance from the start of the walk and will prove a keen distraction. They do not feature in this route, however, which opts for an exploration of the surrounding countryside before descending to the quiet village of Merthyr Mawr. You can always play in the sand after the walk.

Sand dunes are notoriously difficult to walk on, and the same is true of the early stages of this walk, which begins along a sandy path into mixed woodland from the parking area at Candleston. (As you enter the parking area, bear right to locate the trail.)

At a path junction, keep forward onto a stony track that rises to a T-junction. Turn right and walk up to Candleston Farm **A**, and there bear left between farm buildings to locate a double gate giving onto a wide, wall track. Turn onto this and then follow it left to enter a large arable field.

Immediately, turn right along the field edge, following the boundary wall of Coed Cwintin which is a habitat much favoured by pheasants that can start up with alarming noise if caught unawares by your approach.

St Teilo's Church, Merthyr Mawr

PUBLIC TRANSPORT Buses to Ogmore-by-Sea
REFRESHMENTS Pub in Ogmore-by-Sea
PUBLIC TOILETS At start
ORDNANCE SURVEY MAPS Landranger 170 (Vale of Glamorgan), Explorer 151 (Cardiff & Bridgend)

Beyond a gate, where the woodland wall changes direction, go half-right across the ensuing field. The start of the path from the gate is not easy to locate, but the route heads for a gap ahead in what remains of a mature hawthorn hedgerow. Go through the gap and continue into the next field, as if aiming for the far right-hand corner. But, on drawing level with a wooden gate in a fence on the right, double back to the right, following a path alongside the fence, now on the left **B**. This leads to a step-stile in a field corner, once more at the edge of Coed Cwintin.

Merthyr Mawr is a small and pleasant village on the right bank of the River Ogmore. A part of the parish of Ogmore is occupied by sand dunes, but its name probably derives from its elevated position.

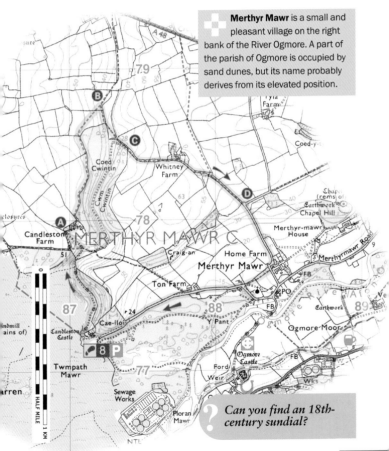

Can you find an 18th-century sundial?

Farmland, Merthyr Mawr

Over the stile, bear right into a pasture, but then cut across to the far left-hand corner, and there go through the hedgerow into the next field, where there is a step-stile on the right, beside a gate. Cross this, once more following the woodland boundary on the right, heading up the field. On the way, you may spot some outstanding fungal growths at the base of a mature ash tree. Keep on past this, heading up the field until it becomes possible to bear right into the course of an obvious old track **C**. Turn up this track towards Whitney Farm.

Keep forward, to the right of the farm, and then leave on the farm access, which leads out to meet a surfaced lane at a U-bend **D**. Bear right, descending, into Merthyr Mawr. At the edge of the village, the road bears right and left.

Immediately after the left bend, leave the road by turning right over a stone stile onto a signposted path across a rough pasture. On the far side, cross another stile from where the path continues through a short stretch of woodland to emerge onto a road. The way back to the start lies down the road ahead, but for a moment divert left to visit the parish church of St Teilo which has some interesting gravestones in a shelter at the back of the church.

Having visited the church, go back up the road and bear left, following the road, *taking care against approaching traffic*, for half a mile (800m) back to the start. ●

Margam

9

START Margam Country Park
DISTANCE 3 miles (5km)
TIME 2 hours
PARKING Margam Country Park (charge)
ROUTE FEATURES Woodland trails; hill tracks; farmland trails; surfaced pathways

The inspiration that turned the grounds of Margam Castle into a country park for the benefit of all has done wonders to rejuvenate an important centre in the history of Wales. The country park, with its aviary, miniature railway and boating lake, is immensely popular with children, and rightly so, but this walk elects to explore the hillsides above, offering chance sightings of the red and fallow deer herds that occupy the estate.

Margam Abbey was founded in 1147 on the site of a Celtic monastery, one of the greatest in Wales. At the Dissolution it was bought by the Mansel family and passed down the family line. The present castle, which is grandly mock-Tudor, was built between 1830 and 1835 for Christopher Mansel Talbot, MP for Glamorgan from 1830 until 1890, and '**Father of the House of Commons**' from 1874.

The Millennium Gnome

Start from the visitor centre at the right-hand end of the castle by walking past three large boulders to gain a gated trail to the left of a

PUBLIC TRANSPORT Buses to entrance of country park
REFRESHMENTS Café in visitor centre
PUBLIC TOILETS At start
ORDNANCE SURVEY MAPS Landranger 170 (Vale of Glamorgan), Explorer 165 Swansea)

stone building. Go through a tall gate and onto a number of waymarked trails. This walk follows the green trail, and is waymarked throughout, but you may need to keep your eyes open to spot some of the waymark poles where the route deviates from the obvious route. The rule is simple: whenever the track forks, follow the green waymarks.

A short way beyond the gate, the track forks. Branch left as the path runs alongside a narrow watercourse, a man-made leat used to supply water to the castle. The path rises steadily and soon passes (to the left) a small hillock, Mynydd y Castell, which is the site of an Iron Age hill-fort.

The track soon curves round **A** to enter Cwm Philip, a lovely wooded valley with open hill slopes on the right. The mix of trees here is good – rowan, holly, willow, birch, ash and hawthorn – and provides a ready source of year-round food for the birds that inhabit the woodlands. Gradually, the track climbs towards a gate. Just before

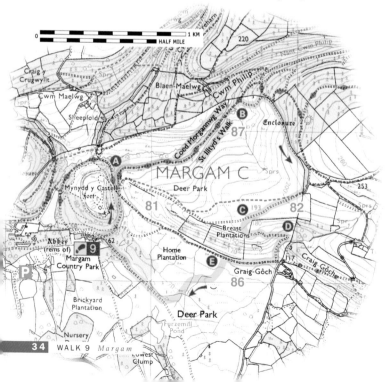

Margam Castle

this, branch right **B** onto a steeply ascending stony track through bracken, which soon follows the estate boundary wall, believed to have been built in the 16th century primarily to define the Mansel Estate, but also to keep in what was then a newly-acquired herd of deer.

You can still see deer today; the herd is mainly red and fallow deer, and they roam freely across the estate. If you are quiet and approach slowly you may be able to get quite close to them. They are accustomed to having people around them, but won't take any chances – and nor should you, especially during the autumn rut, when the stags are romantically inclined, and will see off anything they consider a threat. *Keep well clear of the deer at this time.*

The path climbs to a deer gate, after which it continues along the boundary, still climbing for a little while longer. The high point is a good place to see if you can spot any buzzards and affords a spectacular panoramic view. From here, a grassy track descends to a waymark pole that stands along a

> **?** *What was special about the way the monks of Margam extracted coal from the mine?*

conspicuous trail across the pasture; this is an old drove road that used to pass through the estate.

Bear right onto the drove road, but part way down, keep an eye open for a waymark pole on the left **C** where the route leaves the main descending track and swings left to a lower waymark. There, it goes left again to descend through swathes of bracken.

As the track descends see if you can spot the entrance to a level into the Monks' Mine on the left **D**. The mine could be more than 700 years old and was first worked by the monks of Margam Abbey.

Eventually, the track winds down to intercept a lower track. Turn right, but after about 330 yds (300m), leave the ongoing track at a waymark **E** and branch left into a large open pasture. Then bear right to a waymark pole in midfield and walk on to intercept a broad stony track alongside a deer fence. Bear left and follow the track down to meet a surfaced estate road.

Turn right and follow the estate road back to the start.

Margam Country Park

Cwm Carn and Twmbarlwm

START	Cwm Carn Visitor Centre
DISTANCE	3¼ miles (5.3km)
TIME	2 hours
PARKING	Car park at visitor centre
ROUTE FEATURES	Woodland trails (some steep); lakeside paths; open mountain tops

There is a good deal of steep climbing to do in this walk, but the effort is well rewarded. With little to stand in the way, the views are extensive and reach to the Brecon Beacons in one direction and the coast of north Devon in the other. The highest point is crowned with both an ancient hill-fort and a Norman motte and bailey castle.

Begin from the car park and walk towards the visitor centre, passing to its right to go through a gate onto a surfaced path above Nant Carn. The path soon enters the shade of trees – beech, ash and oak – then leaves the shade as it moves up towards the edge of Nantcarn Lake. Cross a footbridge on the right, and continue round the lake.

At the far side, go forward through a wooden chicane, onto another woodland path beside an in-flowing stream. Soon, pass a small pond, and, a short way on, at a staging post for the Numeracy Trail, bear right, up steps, to gain an ascending path that leads up to join a broad track near a metal gate. Turn right and walk on as far as a metal gate. Beyond this, turn immediately left through a bridlegate onto another ascending path. At the next path junction, turn sharply right to continue ascending.

The path now climbs to meet a surfaced forest road (signpost for the Raven Walk). Turn right along the road, but only as far as a nearby hairpin bend. Here, leave the road

PUBLIC TRANSPORT None
REFRESHMENTS Restaurant at visitor centre
PUBLIC TOILETS At visitor centre
ORDNANCE SURVEY MAPS Landranger 171 (Cardiff & Newport); Explorer 152 (Newport & Pontypool)

by heading right, onto a broad forest track towards a barrier. But, only a short way on, leave the track by branching left onto a waymarked bridleway **A** – the continuation of the Raven Walk – which now climbs very steeply through the woodland.

At the top, the path reaches another forest road at a gathering of junctions. Take the highest of three roads and walk up to Pegwn-y-bwlch **B**. Continue to a step-stile and start climbing on a path signposted to Castle Mound. The steep uphill leg-work continues for a while longer.

Eventually, however, the gradient eases as the path passes through the outer ditches of the hill-fort. Through the ditches, follow the ongoing path to reach the triangulation pillar that adorns the summit.

Not far away, you will see a large mound. This is the 'motte' of a motte and bailey castle. Now head towards it.

Twmbarlwm Mound is a Norman motte and bailey castle built in the 12th and 13th centuries to control the high ground and surrounding area. It stands on the eastern flank of a rock-cut ditch and encloses about 12 acres (5 ha). It is thought to be an Iron Age hill-fort, but may be of medieval construction. There is the possibility, too, that it was used as a beacon hill to signal danger in times of trouble.

Cwmcarn Lake

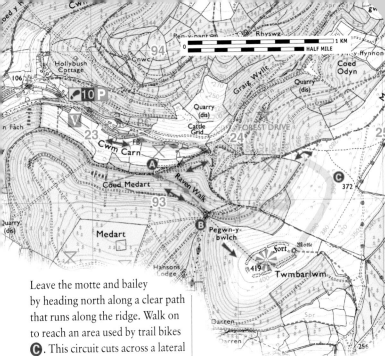

Leave the motte and bailey by heading north along a clear path that runs along the ridge. Walk on to reach an area used by trail bikes **C**. This circuit cuts across a lateral path. Turn left onto the path, taking care if any trail bikers are about.

Follow the path through bracken to reach a fence corner bounding a young plantation. Now follow the path as it parallels the plantation boundary. The path descends, never far from the boundary of the plantation, but becomes increasingly overgrown with bracken in summer.

Lower down, the path swings to the left and starts to rise. Follow this briefly, until a fenceline appears on the right within which an area of plantation has been clear felled. When path and fence almost meet, leave the path by turning right through bracken and walking down an indistinct path, never far from the fence. Descend beside the fence, ducking beneath an established beech tree, and continue down to meet two step-stiles. Cross these onto a surfaced forest road and turn left.

? *Can you find a wooden shepherd?*

Shepherd and dog

Now follow the forest road, passing a large children's play area, and heading back to Pegwn-y-bwlch. Here, turn onto the signposted Raven Walk and descend steeply through the woods encountered on the way up. On reaching the broad forest trail, turn right to the hairpin bend. Keep left and, a short way on, reach another Raven Walk signpost. Branch left here, retracing the outward route.

An alternative finish (unsuitable for young children) exists from the broad forest trail, adding little or nothing to the overall distance. Instead of turning right to the hairpin bend, keep left, passing a barrier and continuing along the broad trail for about 900 yds (800m) to reach a step-stile on the right giving onto a very steep set of steps that lead down to another step-stile. Over this, a very steep descent follows, dropping as a narrow path through bilberries and heather, and finally reaching a surfaced path in the valley below, a short distance from a car park. Turn right towards the car park, but then veer left onto a path that leads quickly back to the visitor centre. ●

Motte, Twmbarlwm

Mynydd Maen Common

This is a very easy walk to the summit of a heathery hill that commands far-reaching views. The route is uncomplicated, and although the landscape is marred by electricity pylons, this scarcely seems to matter – here the views are everything.

START Edge of Mynydd Maen Common
DISTANCE 3½ miles (5.6km)
TIME 2 hours
PARKING Area at edge of common
ROUTE FEATURES Moorland and upland paths and tracks

11

🥾 Begin from the parking area by turning right and following the road for about 330 yds (300m) to reach the edge of a huge plantation Ⓐ. Turn left to follow the plantation edge for ½ mile (800m), and, when it bends abruptly to the right, walk away from a wall corner, striking out across open moorland and roughly targeting the two radio masts in the distance. By moving a little to the left, you will soon intercept a clear path across the heather moorland. Keep an eye open for a large marker stone which defines the boundary, as defined by an Act of Parliament in 1839, between two mineral operators.

Boundary stone

PUBLIC TRANSPORT None
REFRESHMENTS Pubs in Newbridge and Abercarn
PUBLIC TOILETS None on route
ORDNANCE SURVEY MAPS Landranger 171 (Cardiff & Newport); Explorer 152 (Newport & Pontypool)

The **birdlife** is what you would expect from this lofty landscape – kestrels, buzzards, meadow pipits, summertime swallows and swifts and the occasional wheatear. Blue and coal tits populate the plantation from where willow warblers call. But this is a popular habitat, too, for butterflies including the small heath, gatekeeper, meadow brown, red admirals and a few speckled wood.

Follow the moorland path until it intercepts a service track for the radio masts **B**, and turn right onto this, heading towards the masts. As you approach the masts, bear right to pass the compound, and then strike a little to the left, following a stony path across the moorland. When this forks, branch right, and soon reach the triangulation pillar that marks the summit.

The view from the top of the hill – Mynydd Twyn-glas – is quite extensive and embraces the distant Brecon Beacons, including Pen y Fan and Corn Du, Sugar Loaf and Skirrid Fawr above Abergavenny and the wide sweep of the Mouth of the Severn to the south. The whole of the summit plateau is swathed in rich heather during the summertime, and is a delight to behold.

Heather moorland

Retreat from the summit by heading back towards the radio masts. Go past them, and stay along the service track which provides delightfully easy walking at a gently descending gradient. When you reach the surfaced road, turn left to return to the start. ●

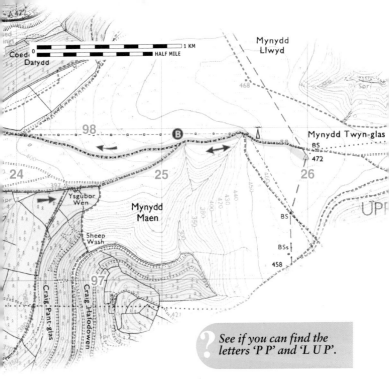

Mynydd
Llwyd

Coed
Datydd

Mynydd Twyn-glas

Mynydd
Maen

Ysgubor
Wen

Sheep
Wash

Craig-Pant-glas

Craig Halodowen

UPP

See if you can find the letters 'P P' and 'L U P'.

Mynydd Maen Common

12 *Dare Valley*

START Cwmdare
DISTANCE 3½ miles
(5.6km)
TIME 2 hours
PARKING Dare Valley
Country Park Visitor
Centre
ROUTE FEATURES Upland
paths; some ascent

To a casual eye Dare Valley reveals nothing of the coal-mining activity that went on here. Nature has largely reclaimed the spoil heaps – with a little help from man – and only a few items of pithead gear remain as memorials to the hardy men who worked the coal faces. The walk is a simple loop, climbing steadily up to the head of Cwm Darren and there circling above spectacular cliffs before making an easy descent. The views northwards embrace the Brecon Beacons and the higher part of the walk touches on the moorland across the high ground.

Set off from the visitor centre and walk to the right along the access road as far as a signposted turning on the left for the Coed Morgannwg Way. A wide path immediately starts climbing between hedgerows that are popular with a wide range of butterflies. The gradient is nowhere unduly demanding, but the earlier stages are steeper than what follows.

Soon, the gradient eases as the route continues through bracken, passing a group of derelict houses **A**, continuing then up to a step-stile and gate. Beyond this, the path continues as a grassy track above Craig Pen-rhiw-llech. As the path climbs, so the views improve, and this is a good place to keep an eye open for soaring buzzards or the high-speed flight of a peregrine falcon.

PUBLIC TRANSPORT Buses to Cwmdare
REFRESHMENTS Café in visitor centre
PUBLIC TOILETS At start
ORDNANCE SURVEY MAPS Landranger 170 (Vale of Glamorgan), Explorer 166 (Rhondda & Merthyr Tydfil)

The path rises steadily to overlook the impressive crags at Tarren y Bwllfa. When the on-going path forks **B**, branch right following a good path above the crags. A short way on this forks again, near a white-topped marker stone, where the walk leaves the company of the Coed Morgannwg Way.

Simply keep following a clear on-going path beyond the end of the crags, where the path slants across the slopes of Cefn y Llethr Hir before turning down through the bracken of Craig y Bwllfa to reach

For many young boys leaving school in the 1950s, **coal-mining** was one of a limited number of options. Many pits were closed in the 1980s, and today throughout South Wales, the valleys show little sign of an industry that dominated not only people's lives, but the whole area, too.

a gate and step-stile. Over this, continue descending and, at a waymark where the path forks, branch left through more bracken and continue down to reach a field gate **C**.

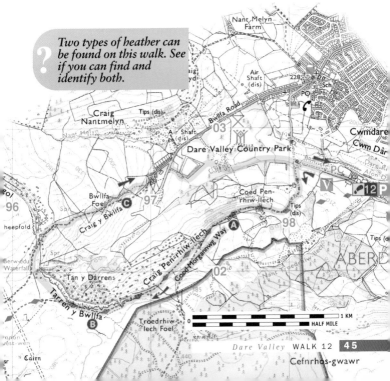

Two types of heather can be found on this walk. See if you can find and identify both.

Through the gate, bear right, descending on an indistinct path initially close by a fence on the right, but then striking away towards a solitary telegraph pole in mid-field. Head down for a step-stile at the bottom of the hill slope. Over the stile, bear left to another and then continue forward to pass in front of a row of terrace houses.

Having passed the terrace, turn right onto a lower road and, after a few strides, turn left again, leaving the road for a clear track heading back into the country park. Soon, the path reaches a reservoir. Turn left over a footbridge to pass it and then continue down on a stony track before cutting across a corner near pithead gear to go forward towards another lake. Bear right towards a metal barrier and from it head left onto a path along the edge of the lake, which is popular with moorhens and their young.

Cross a footbridge over the outflow and turn immediately right to parallel a stream flanked by luxurious growths of alder and soon reach the road leading back to the Dare Valley Centre. ●

Cwm Dare

Cardiff and the Taff

13

DISTANCE 3½ miles (5.6km)
TIME 2 hours
PARKING Alongside the A470; on-street parking in side roads is free on Sundays
ROUTE FEATURES Parkland paths and walks

There are times on this walk when you have no idea how close you are to a major city centre. The route skirts Cardiff Castle – the entrance is nearby – and follows a dock feeder stream as far as the River Taff before looping around Pontcanna playing fields and heading back to the city centre. It doesn't really matter where you start, but the entrance to Bute Park has been used here as it is only a short walk from the city centre.

? *Who opened Cardiff Bridge, and when?*

Weir, River Taff

Walk through the archway giving into Bute Park and go forward along the driveway. Take the first main turning on the right to pass a circle of standing stones, a Gorsedd Circle, at which Eisteddfods are proclaimed. Walk towards the rear facade of Cardiff Castle and then bear left on a track that leads past the castle to enter Bute Park Arboretum.

PUBLIC TRANSPORT Rail and bus services to Cardiff
REFRESHMENTS Numerous places nearby in Cardiff centre
PUBLIC TOILETS None on route
ORDNANCE SURVEY MAPS Landranger 171 (Cardiff & Newport), Explorer 151 (Cardiff & Bridgend)

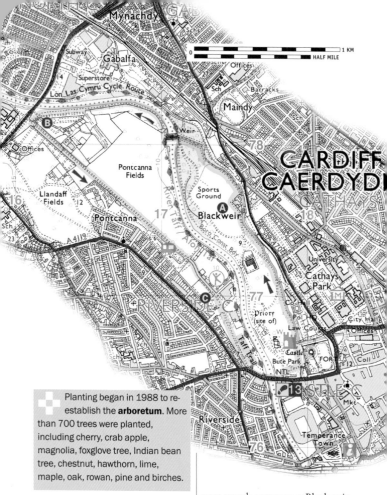

Planting began in 1988 to re-establish the **arboretum**. More than 700 trees were planted, including cherry, crab apple, magnolia, foxglove tree, Indian bean tree, chestnut, hawthorn, lime, maple, oak, rowan, pine and birches.

At the far side of the castle, at a cross-track, keep forward, but bear slightly right to gain a path alongside a feeder stream.

Follow the streamside path, passing a footbridge, and go on until it reaches the edge of playing fields, near a park entrance at Blackweir **A**. Here, bear left to pass in front of the changing rooms and, having passed them, bear right to continue trekking around the park boundary. In the far corner of the field, go forward into woodland, on a broad path, and shortly reach a weir on the River Taff.

Cross the weir and immediately bear right to pass a metal gate and barrier and so gain a path alongside a fence, which soon runs along the banks of the Taff.

Follow the path, which eventually comes out near a main road, but bears left to a gate and barrier **B**. Turn immediately left and go through the gates into Pontcanna Fields. Now simply keep forward down a long avenue of trees, keeping an eye open for occasional grey squirrels.

Stay on the main drive, which later passes the Glamorgan County Cricket Grounds **C** beyond which the path leads into Sophia Gardens, before running out to meet the main road into Cardiff. Turn left to cross Cardiff Bridge and so complete the walk. ●

River Taff, Cardiff

14 *Sirhowy Valley*

START Near Crosskeys
DISTANCE 3¾ miles (6km)
TIME 2 hours
PARKING Car park at entrance to country park
ROUTE FEATURES Woodland trails; railway trackbed

All the terrain covered in this walk and much of the adjoining land, too, was once the scene of considerable industrial activity. It is hard to see all that now, so successfully has Nature clawed back what was once hers. The first half of the walk makes use of an old railway trackbed, while the return from the Ynys Hywel Centre passes through excellent woodland for spotting birds.

Set off from the Full Moon car park, and walk along the former railway trackbed.

Full Moon Cottage and the old signal box opposite are all that survived the closure of the Sirhowy railway line in 1970. Now the line is flanked by semi-natural woodland, comprising beech, ash, oak, elm, alder and sycamore, and this plays host to a wealth of birdlife, more than 40 breeding species in fact, including pied flycatcher, wood warbler, redstart, great spotted and green woodpeckers. You will almost certainly catch sight, too, of buzzards either patrolling the skies above or perched on a branch.

PUBLIC TRANSPORT Buses to park entrance
REFRESHMENTS Seasonal coffee shop Ynys Hywel Centre
PUBLIC TOILETS At start
ORDNANCE SURVEY MAPS Landranger 171 (Cardiff & Newport), Explorer 166 (Rhondda & Merthyr Tydfil)

Continue along the surfaced trackbed to reach another car park at Nine Mile Point **Ⓐ**.

Continue beyond the car park and adjacent picnic area until it meets a surfaced lane. Turn left, climbing steeply for a short while to reach the Ynys Hywel Centre **Ⓑ**.

The Ynys Hywel Centre, which specialises in private and corporate functions, was developed from a 17th-century farmhouse, and opened in its present form in 1990. There is an excellent restaurant here serving Sunday lunches and a seasonal coffee shop.

The car park takes its name from the wording of the Monmouthshire Canal Act of 1802, which permitted the Tredegar Iron Company to build a **tramway** from Tredegar to a point nine miles from Newport; this is roughly where the car park is today. There used to be a station here, too, but that was closed in 1960. But before the nationalisation of the railways in 1947, the Great Western Railway and the London and North Western Railway met here. Beyond **Nine Mile Point**, there used to be four sets of railway tracks, such was the extent of the railway system here.

? *What was unique about the Ynys Hywel Camping Barn?*

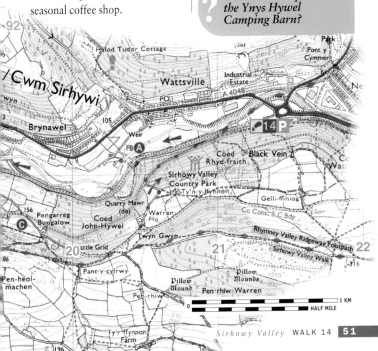

Sirhowy Valley Country Park

Just near the entrance to the centre, turn left up steps onto the Raven Walk. After the initial flight of steps, bear left along a grassy path to the Ynys Hywel Camping Barn.

Go past the camping barn, following an undulating path that steadily climbs to intercept a broad, stony track. Turn left.

Just along this section of the forest track, notice how a lot of the adjacent alder has self-seeded to provide new growth beside the trail. The woodland above is Graig Goch, now largely pine, Japanese larch, oak and beech. There used to be much charcoal production here in the last two centuries, and large areas of trees were felled to feed the iron works.

Continue along the trail, going past a branching trail on the right (the continuation of the Raven Walk), and keep on, ignoring all side paths, until eventually, just beyond a barrier, it reaches a surfaced lane **C**.

Turn right, but immediately take the lower of two routes, a rough track heading towards a barrier and into a larch plantation. When the track forks, keep forward, descending along the forest trail until, as it bears to the right, you can leave it by branching left onto a steeply descending, loose stone path going down through woodland. Ignore side turnings, and keep following the same path to emerge back at the Full Moon car park.

Afan Country Park

START Cynonville
DISTANCE 3¾ miles (6km)
TIME 2 hours
PARKING Car parks at start
ROUTE FEATURES Woodland trails; moorland paths

15

Afan Country Park is set in the picturesque Afan Valley and has a variety of woodland from conifer plantations to native broadleaved. This presents an excellent opportunity for many different species of birds, mammals, insects and plants to thrive. This walk wanders into the woods alongside a tributary of the Afan, the Nant Cynon, finally leaving the woodlands behind for an airy stretch of moorland that concludes with an ancient valley road. Keep an eye open for the fallow deer that browse among the higher conifer plantations.

It is hard to believe that this now lovely valley was once a focal point of much industry. Mature woodlands now soften the landscape, concealing abandoned mines and tramways. Rivers and streams that were once choked with coal dust now run clear. **Adders** can occasionally be found basking in the sun around the fields in the valley bottom and a good range of butterflies frequent the sunnier spots. There is a good variety of birdlife, too, from redstarts and blackcaps to dippers and woodpeckers, even nightjar have been heard in the young plantations.

From the cafe and visitor centre bear left (or right as you look at the centre) onto the signposted forest trails, many of which are shared with cyclists on expensive bikes that, alas, have no bells, *so take care.*

Museum exhibits

PUBLIC TRANSPORT Buses to Cynonville
REFRESHMENTS Café in the country park
PUBLIC TOILETS At start
ORDNANCE SURVEY MAPS Landranger 170 (Vale of Glamorgan), Explorer 166 (Rhondda & Merthyr Tydfil)

Follow a constructed path round to a bench and near this go down a few steps onto the red waymarked trail. At the bottom of the steps, turn left onto an ascending track. Continue up to a track junction and go forward leaving the red route and continuing farther into the forest, ignoring side turnings.

At a path junction, bear right, continuing to follow the main thrust of the valley, passing along below walls densely covered with moss.

? *Can you find a wooden buzzard?*

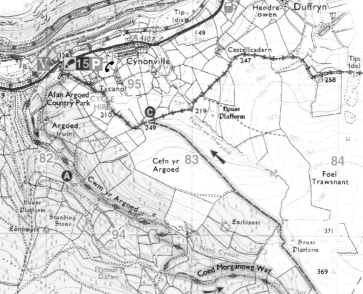

Wild flowers

At the next major cross-track, near cycle trail post P4, bear to the right, descending to meet a broader trail, and now joining the Coed Morgannwg Way **A**. Turn left, and contine alongside the Nant Cynon.

The trail climbs steadily and crosses the stream. Higher up, it loops around as it heads up to the top edge of the forest. When the forest trail arrives at a T-junction, turn left at cycle trail post P6. Descend gently, still on the Coed Morgannwg Way, and continue up to the top edge of the forest.

There, turn left and keep forward for about 220 yds (200m), and then, as the main trail bears to the right to run along a forest edge, leave it by branching left to a metal gate and stile **B**.

Over the stile, keep forward on a broad grassy track, heading for the top edge of the forest. Continue along the obvious track, which passes through an area of mining spoil (although it is hard to detect), and twice passing along the forest boundary.

From the end of the second stretch of forest, the track continues forward over an area of open land known as Cefn yr Argoed. Continue down beside a fence to meet an old track  **C**, the old parish road, which was the main road in the valley for hundreds of years, until about 1920. It is a delight to see these ancient highways threading a way across what would have been very inhospitable, and possibly dangerous, countryside.

The walk meets the old parish road near a couple of metal gates; go through the right-hand one and continue descending. Eventually, the track leads down to a cottage at the head of a surfaced lane. Go forward, still descending, but after about 160 yds (150m), leave the lane and branch left onto a stony track (red waymark). Walk on to reach a building and then, by it, turn right, down steps and pass behind the visitor centre to complete the walk.

Evening light, Cwm Afan

Craig y Llyn

16

START A4061 above Llyn Fawr, Hirwaun

DISTANCE 4¼ miles (7km)

TIME 2 hours

PARKING Area above Llyn Fawr, A4061

ROUTE FEATURES Woodland trails

This walk is all about woodland trails and the peaceful atmosphere that permeates pine plantations. Of course, the view across Llyn Fawr to Craig y Llyn, which is quite stunning, also helps, but essentially this easy walk is an excuse to wander broad trails and listen to the sound of woodland birds. It also provides the opportunity to visit the highest summit in Glamorgan.

Set off from the parking area alongside the A4061 and, *taking care against approaching traffic*, walk back up the road for a short distance, as far as a bridleway waymark and there leave the road for a grassy path on the right, alongside a fence. The path runs on to intercept a broad track. Turn right and press on as far as a signpost. Here, the path forks. Branch left and climb a little as the path bends up towards the edge of the plantation above.

Craig y Llyn

PUBLIC TRANSPORT None

REFRESHMENTS Pubs in Hirwaun and Treherbert

PUBLIC TOILETS None on route

ORDNANCE SURVEY MAPS Landranger 170 (Vale of Glamorgan), Explorer 166 (Rhondda & Merthyr Tydfil)

Pass through a metal gate and then keep forward now following the waymarked Coed Morgannwg Way, a 33-mile (53k) route from Aberdare to Margam Country Park, near Swansea.

At a cross-track **A** keep forward and then, when you reach a track on the left **B** that leads up to a radio mast, turn left for a few minutes to reach the triangulation point on an unnamed summit above Craig y Llyn. This innocuous summit is the highest point in Glamorgan; would that it could be more glamorous. Return to the main track. *If you want to shorten the walk, you can continue beyond the triangulation pillar to intercept the longer route at Point* **D**.

Back on the main track, the route is splendidly simple, and the birdlife increasingly noticeable as you move farther from the road. After ½ mile (800m) the track starts to make a pronounced bend to the left, near a large yellow pole. Keep going, and eventually emerge onto a very broad forest trail at a U-bend, near a signpost **C**.

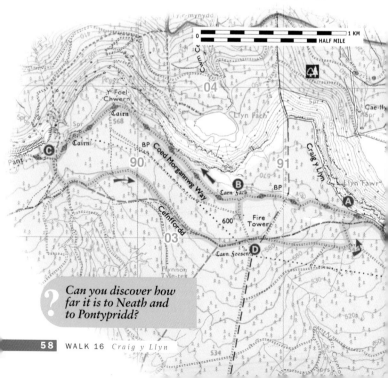

? *Can you discover how far it is to Neath and to Pontypridd?*

Craig y Llyn, Rhondda

Turn left, and follow the trail, which descends gently, to a T-junction. Go left again, soon passing a large clear-felled area around which the forest trail skirts, offering improving views beyond the forest to distant hills.

At a cross-junction **D**, the radio tower at the triangulation pillar visited earlier is a short way up to the left. *Anyone taking the shorter route will rejoin the main route here.*

Keep forward at the cross-track, and at a bridleway sign farther on. The trail now descends gently. At the next main junction, turn left and walk up until you encounter the bridleway (blue waymark) again. This time, turn right, leaving the main trail, and turning onto the bridleway, which is followed through a wide firebreak until it meets the early part of the forest trail used on the outward section.

Go right, and follow the descending track as it curves left and then right, passing a signpost and returning along the outward route.

17 *Ogmore-by-Sea*

START Ogmore-by-Sea
DISTANCE 4½ miles (7.2km)
TIME 2½ hours
PARKING Car park above foreshore (charge)
ROUTE FEATURES Coastal paths; farm tracks and lanes; riverside path

The coastline south of Porthcawl is especially beautiful and greatly popular with crowds of visitors on a warm day. The beauty of this walk lies in the easy strolling along the coastline, after which it turns inland and crosses to an unsuspected valley before returning alongside the Ogmore River, the Afon Ogwr. Without causing too much difficulty, this walk can easily be combined with Walk 1 (Dunraven Bay) to give a slightly longer outing.

Set off from the coastal car park near the Pen-y-Bont Surf Life Saving Club and head past the public toilets, and then keep on in the same direction along the coast. Soon, pass through a gate to continue along the foreshore with lovely displays of rock formations to add interest to the early part of the walk.

> *Part way down the Pant Mari Flanders there is a curious stone structure. Can you figure out what its purpose is?*

The on-going path, founded on springy turf, simply follows the coastline, and eventually approaches steeper cliffs and a dry inlet from the sea **A** just after warning signs about the caves and cliffs. Keep to the highest path along this stretch, and this will feed you into the inlet and a wide grassy valley leading to a road at the top. Turn right, following the road towards West Farm. Keep to the right of the farm, rejoining the road a short way on, just as it bears left towards Southerndown.

PUBLIC TRANSPORT Buses to Ogmore-by-Sea
REFRESHMENTS Hotel and small café in Ogmore
PUBLIC TOILETS At start
ORDNANCE SURVEY MAPS Landranger 170 (Vale of Glamorgan), Explorer 151 (Cardiff & Bridgend)

Walk up the road as far as a cattle-grid (110 yds/100m) **B**, and there branch left, leaving the road by turning onto a signposted bridleway (blue waymark) between walls. The path narrows down and is seasonally overgrown with nettles, brambles and bracken and leads to a gate. Turn right after this onto a broad grassy path that leads out to a road. Cross into the lane opposite, signposted for Heol-y-mynydd.

Ogmore gazes out into the vast expanse of the Bristol Channel, a major thoroughfare used by shipping heading for Bristol, Swansea or Cardiff. But from time to time the waters are visited by **bottle-nosed dolphins**. They have a short but distinct beak and a tall dorsal fin centrally placed.

Coastline, Ogmore-by-Sea

River Ogmore

The lane leads on to a large open common area **C**. Cross the road and go forward onto a very wide grassy path, but almost immediately bear left through bracken onto a track that heads for Pant Mari Flanders.

A short way on, as the grassy path forks, branch left, descending into the valley, and then follow the main path.

A number of paths lead down the valley, which from time to time divide and then converge, but keep following the main thrust of the valley, until the valley itself splits,

with Pant Norton on the left and Pant y Cwteri on the right. Bear right, following a clear path that later becomes a stony vehicle track and leads out to the road.

Turn left onto the main road, but leave it almost immediately by moving onto grass-covered sandy pastures on the right **D**, gradually drifting across towards the River Ogmore following a surfaced lane towards a cottage. Just on reaching it, bear left onto a clear path, initially through bracken, but from which it soon breaks free to run parallel with the river.

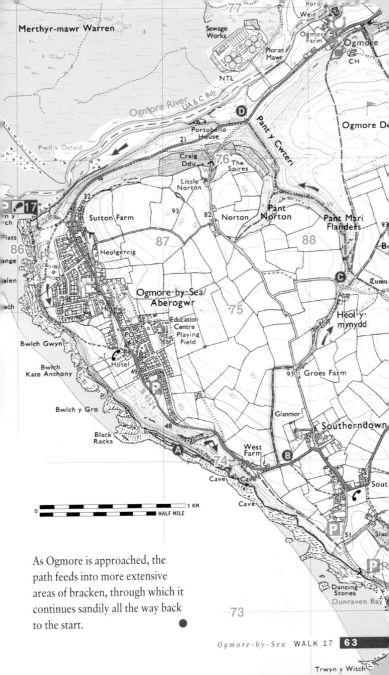

As Ogmore is approached, the
path feeds into more extensive
areas of bracken, through which it
continues sandily all the way back
to the start.

18 *Nash Point and St Donat's*

START Nash Point
DISTANCE 4½ miles (7.2km)
TIME 2½ hours
PARKING Nash Point (£1 charge)
ROUTE FEATURES Clifftop paths, roads, woodland paths, farm fields

The cliffs either side of Nash Point are quite spectacular – and crumbling, so don't get too close. The vegetation above the cliffs is hugely popular with butterflies, while the cliffs provide a haven for sheltering sea birds. The walk also visits the ancient castle and Norman church at St Donat's, as well as the Norman church in Marcross. The walking is generally easy, but close control will need to be exercised over children along the clifftops.

From the parking area walk to the right of the refreshment kiosk and out to the cliff edge, there bearing left towards the lighthouses, *taking care not to encroach too closely to the cliff edge.*

At the first lighthouse, turn in through a gate to walk around the lighthouse, then continuing to the huge foghorns and the second light. Beyond, a stone stile takes you out of the lighthouse grounds and back onto the coastal path.

A public outcry in 1832 followed the loss of 40 lives when the passenger steamer *Frolic* ran aground on Nash Point sandbank. Two lighthouse towers were built exactly 1,000 ft (305m) apart and carefully positioned so they could be aligned by ships sailing up the Bristol Channel.

Now simply follow the coastal path, which eventually reaches a stile giving into a narrow strip of woodland. Follow a clear path through this. The woodland contains some lovely spreads of

PUBLIC TRANSPORT Buses to Marcross and St Donat's
REFRESHMENTS Refreshment kiosk at Nash Point
PUBLIC TOILETS None on route
ORDNANCE SURVEY MAPS Landranger 170 (Vale of Glamorgan), Explorer 151 (Cardiff & Bridgend)

ground ivy and hart's tongue fern, as well as a ruined, ivy-clad, chimney, which probably belonged to the barracks that used to be here. When the path forks, branch right, and finally go down steps to reach a concrete promenade in front of a castellated building Ⓐ.

Go across the promenade and the slipway, turning, on the far side, up four steps to gain a path that ascends briefly into scrubby woodland. On the other side of this, the familiar coastal path resumes as it passes around the edge of a large pasture. Soon, another short stretch of woodland scrub is encountered, after which a stile gives into large fields that commemorate King George V. Over the stile, turn immediately left and walk up the side of first one and then a second field to pass through a metal kissing-gate in a wall at the top corner, onto the St Donat's–Llantwit road Ⓑ.

Turn left, soon reaching the entrance to St Donat's Atlantic College, but ignore this entrance and continue along the road, *taking care against approaching traffic*, for another 330 yds (300m), until you can turn sharply left to pass through a metal gate onto a footpath – a college driveway – (signposted) into the grounds of the college Ⓒ.

Lighthouse, Nash Point

The driveway leads to the castle, a 13th-century fortress, which has been lived in continuously since it was built.

> In the early part of the 20th century the castle was acquired by the American newspaper magnate, **William Randolph Hearst**, who made it a centre for antiquities. In its day, it was a popular place with visiting film stars and politicians from Europe and America: Lloyd George attended an Eisteddfod here. Today, it is the home of Atlantic College, an international sixth-form school.

Just before reaching the castle itself, at a car park on the right, bear right down a lane (signposted to St Donat's Church) **D**. The church is of 11th-century construction, and has a beautiful and simple interior design.

Having visited the church, set off back up the lane, but only for a short distance, as far as a signposted turning on the left which gives onto a delightful woodland path. Follow this as it climbs steadily to reach Parc Farm. Go through a rickety gate and immediately turn left over a stile to begin a waymarked route around the farm that leads to a stone stile in a corner.

Coastal farmland

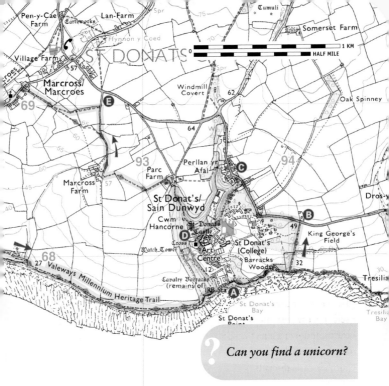

Over the stile, keep forward with a wall on the right for a little over 100 yds (91m), and then cross a step-stile on the right. Head diagonally left across the next field to the far corner where a stile gives into a narrower field. Cross this towards farm buildings to reach an access track at Marcross Farm. Turn right and follow the access out to reach the end of a surfaced lane.

Go forward up the lane for 500 yds (450m), as far as a metal gate on the left **E**. Turn in through this

(waymarked); ignore a field track and go forward along the right-hand edge of the field to another stile in the far corner. For a few strides, maintain the same direction in the next field, then follow the right-hand boundary as it curves to the right. From a waymark, target a large group of trees in the distance (to the right of some white cottages), touching first on a hedgerow corner, and then heading down alongside the hedge to a gate and stile giving onto a hedged track.

Follow the track out as it passes between buildings to reach the Marcross road. Turn left to pass the 12th-century Church of the Holy Trinity – which has an interesting sundial in its grounds, a lepers' 'squint' (now blocked up) below a small window to the right of the porch, and an unusual font.

Continue down the lane until it becomes possible to branch right into a wooded ravine, following a clear path. The ongoing path eventually emerges from the woodland, and goes into the head of Marcross Brook, crossing a couple of in-flowing streams on stepping stones. A short way on, bear left up a broad path to return to the start.

Marcross village is one of a number of villages built about a mile inland along the coast. This could originally have been to offer shelter against coastal gales, or to protect the villages against **Saxon and Viking raiders**. Records show that the land around Marcross was farmed in the 13th century as part of several estates.

Coastline near Nash Point

St Donat's church

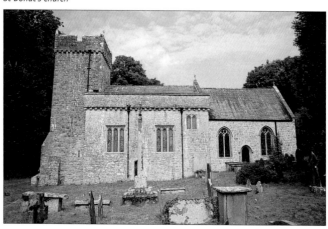

Parc Cwm Darran

START Deri
DISTANCE 5 miles (8.2km)
TIME 3 hours
PARKING Car park at country park
ROUTE FEATURES Woodland trails; lakeside paths; moorland

If ever there was a superb example of how Nature can reclaim the ravages of man's industry it is Parc Cwm Darran. On the site of pithead gear and mining buildings there is now a reed-fringed lake largely covered with yellow water lilies, the hillsides are cloaked in healthy woodlands and it looks for all the world like a natural landscape. This walk takes a look at what man can do with what industry left behind.

Leave the visitor centre and head down towards the lake, keeping to the right of it. The far end of the lake is largely covered with yellow water lilies. In medieval France, the yellow water lily was described as 'the destroyer of pleasure and the poison of love', quite the opposite of an aphrodisiac. Indeed, stonemasons carved the flowers of the water lily into the roof bosses of Westminster Abbey to encourage celibacy.

Go on to the end of the lake, but then keep to the right of a wooden

Parc Cwm Darran

PUBLIC TRANSPORT Buses to entrance
REFRESHMENTS Café at visitor centre
PUBLIC TOILETS At start
ORDNANCE SURVEY MAPS Landranger 171 (Cardiff & Newport), Explorer 166 (Rhondda & Merthyr Tydfil)

The transformation of the **Ogilvie Colliery** is now complete. The pit was closed in February 1975, and work began the following autumn to reclaim the site. More than 1.5 million tonnes of colliery waste was remoulded to blend in with the surrounding hillsides, the river scene was improved, all the buildings were demolished, the debris buried and the mineshafts capped. What was the colliery feeder pond has been preserved as a water feature. It is as if someone has waved a magic wand: now rare butterflies are found here, along with dragonflies, damselflies and more than 100 species of bird.

After about 110 yds (100m), leave the lane at a signposted stile on the right **Ⓐ**, and climb initially through bracken and then up a hill slope, keeping roughly in line with the right-hand field boundary to locate another stile among trees. Over this, go forward across a slope on an indistinct path that leads to the boundary of an oak wood, which is appropriate as the village across the valley is called Deri, which in Welsh means 'oak trees'.

Keep on to reach a gate giving into the woodland **Ⓑ**, and through it turn immediately left, climbing steeply on a path that runs

bridge, turning onto a grassy path beside the lake overflow. Keep following the path, which later turns through a neck of woodland to reach another track. Turn left and walk to a surfaced lane, and there turn left again.

? *Can you find a crowned-B?*

Parc Cwm Darran

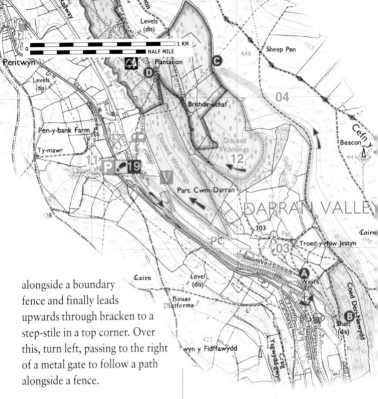

alongside a boundary fence and finally leads upwards through bracken to a step-stile in a top corner. Over this, turn left, passing to the right of a metal gate to follow a path alongside a fence.

For a while the fence line descends, while the path continues to rise gently, but is later rejoined by the fence once beyond Troed-y-rhiw Jestyn Farm. Continue following the path which eventually treks out across open moorland. When the moorland path forks, branch left through bracken. The path runs on to reach the top edge of the country park, and leads on to a stile giving access to the park **C**. Turn left over this onto a permissive path (white waymarks).

The path works a way round to run along the woodland boundary and later descends beside a man-made watercourse. Continue beside this as it swings around the hill slope and heads back towards the woodland. Go as far as a hairpin bend **D**, and there go left with the descending track to drop down to a path not far from Ogilvie Lake. Keep to the right of the lake and, at the far end, cross a footbridge and walk back up to the visitor centre to complete the walk. ●

● Wood and moorland wildlife ● fine views ● butterflies

20 *Craig yr Allt*

START Caerphilly Common

DISTANCE 5½ miles (9km)

TIME 3 hours

PARKING Area on A469

ROUTE FEATURES Undulating trails; some road walking

Craig yr Allt is a minor summit in the scale of things, but everything is relative and this modest lump offers some far-reaching views south over Cardiff, the Mouth of the Severn and Cardiff Bay. The return route begins along a disused railway trackbed and then pursues quiet country lanes, bright in spring with wild flowers and butterflies, before returning across Caerphilly Common.

Set off from the parking area, and cross onto a stony path opposite that ascends easily through bracken onto Caerphilly Common. Immediately, views open up northwards over Caerphilly, and south across the Mouth of the River Severn.

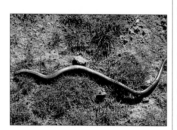

Slow worm

The path crosses the southern edge of Caerphilly Common and, when it swings right to head for the highest point of the common, leave it by branching left (ahead) onto a narrow path across a small hummock, mainly cloaked in bracken but with spreads of common and bell heather to brighten the way.

The path eventually descends to meet a road. Cross this and continue along a path opposite, once more passing through bracken, and heading around the southern edge of Twyn Garwa.

PUBLIC TRANSPORT Rail to Caerphilly; buses along A469

REFRESHMENTS Kiosk at start

PUBLIC TOILETS None on route

ORDNANCE SURVEY MAPS Landranger 171 (Cardiff & Newport); Explorer 151 (Cardiff & Bridgend)

Craig yr Allt

Follow the path for about 330 yds (300m) and then, as it swings round to head for the top of Twyn Garwa, leave it by branching left onto a narrower path through bracken (seasonally overgrown) and flanked by ash, sycamore, birch and hawthorn.

At the next track junction, keep left at a waymark. Now, descend through trees to reach a road. On reaching the road, immediately turn right onto a broad track beside a cottage, and walk up for a short distance to a step-stile on the left giving into a large paddock. Go forward across the paddock, crossing an intermediate step-stile and continuing down the next field to a signpost beyond which another stile gives onto a lane Ⓐ. Turn right.

Follow the lane for 165 yds (150m), and then leave it by turning abruptly left, heading up the access lane to the Rockwood Riding Centre. As the lane levels, continue to a metal gate and immediately branch right through another gate and onto a stony track through bracken. When the track forks, keep left and set off along a delightful terraced route across the southern flanks of Craig yr Allt. At the next fork, branch right (waymarked), climbing a little to continue the traverse.

Eventually, the track starts to descend towards Taff Vale. On the descent, the track forks at a waymark, branch right and go down a narrow path through dense bracken (seasonally heavily overgrown). Continue following the path downwards in zigzags until it reaches a step-stile beside bridge abutments. Turn right here, and follow a surfaced path as it descends easily, passes an isolated house and soon reaches an access point on the left (at metal barriers) giving onto the Taff Trail, which here occupies the route of a disused railway trackbed.

B Turn right along the surfaced trail, continuing to a point just before a bridge spanning the trackbed. Here, branch left to a metal gate giving onto a rough track. Turn right onto the track and almost immediately go right again

to cross the bridge. Now follow the on-going track, climbing easily in the direction of Bwlch-y-maen Farm, but on reaching the earlier Bramble Cottage, turn sharply left through a fence to access a lovely woodland track.

The on-going path leads through broad-leaved woodland and gives onto a large concreted area. On the far side of the concrete, the woodland walk resumes, now along a surfaced path which moves on to pass the Penrhos Cutting, and not much farther on, at another barrier, reach an old lane.

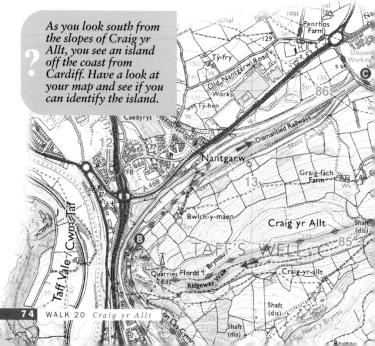

? As you look south from the slopes of Craig yr Allt, you see an island off the coast from Cardiff. Have a look at your map and see if you can identify the island.

C Turn right, and walk up the lane, which parallels a newer road on the left. When the lane reaches a road junction, turn right. Follow the road for about 330 yds (300m), *taking care against approaching traffic*, and then take the first turning on the left, a narrow lane, descending. Go past the entrance to Cwm Farm, and 110 yds (100m) farther on, bear left as the lane now climbs steeply onto the slopes of Twyn Garwa.

Leave the ascending road before its high point, by turning right onto a waymarked path that climbs through a thin strip of woodland, and eventually reaches the edge of Twyn Garwa, where it intercepts a broad path. Turn right, and shortly rejoin the outward route. Keep following the path through bracken and walking out to meet a road.

Cross into a broad track opposite and almost immediately leave it for a waymarked path, retracing the outward route.

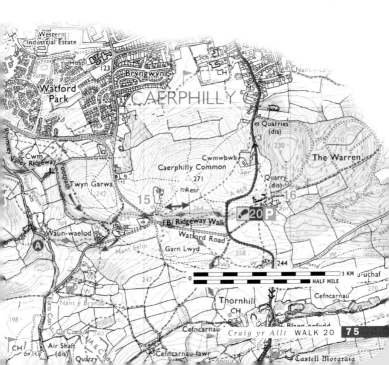

Further Information

Walking Safety

Always take with you both warm and waterproof clothing and sufficient food and drink. Wear suitable footwear, i.e. strong walking boots or shoes that give a good grip over stony ground, on slippery slopes and in muddy conditions. Try to obtain a local weather forecast and bear it in mind before you start. Do not be afraid to abandon your proposed route and return to your starting point in the event of a sudden and unexpected deterioration in the weather.

All the walks described in this book will be safe to do, given due care and respect, even during the winter. Indeed, a crisp, fine winter day often provides perfect walking conditions, with firm ground underfoot and a clarity of light unique to that time of the year.

The most difficult hazard likely to be encountered is mud, especially when walking along woodland and field paths, farm tracks and bridleways - the latter in particular can often get churned up by cyclists and horses. In summer, an additional difficulty may be narrow and overgrown paths, particularly along the edges of cultivated fields. Neither should constitute a major problem provided that the appropriate footwear is worn.

Follow the Country Code

- Enjoy the countryside and respect its life and work
- Guard against all risk of fire
- Take your litter home
- Fasten all gates
- Help to keep all water clean
- Keep your dogs under control
- Protect wildlife, plants and trees
- Keep to public paths across farmland
- Take special care on country roads
- Leave livestock, crops and machinery alone
- Make no unnecessary noise
- Use gates and stiles to cross fences, hedges and walls
    (The Countryside Agency)

Useful Organisations

Council for the Protection of Rural England
128 Southwark Street, London SE1 0SW.
Tel. 020 7981 2800
Fax. 020 7981 2899
E-mail: info@cpre.org.uk
Website: www.cpre.org.uk

Heritage Coast

Countryside Agency
John Dower House, Crescent
Place, Cheltenham GL50 3RA.
Tel. 01242 521381

English Heritage
PO Box 579, Swindon SN2 2YP.
Tel. 0878 333 1181
E-mail: customers@english-
heritage.org.uk; Website:
www.english-heritage.org.uk

English Nature
Northminster House,
Peterborough PE1 1UA.
Tel. 01733 455100
Fax. 01733 455103; E-mail:
enquiries@english-nature.org.uk;
Website: www.english-nature.org.uk

National Trust
Membership and general enquiries:

PO Box 39, Bromley,
Kent BR1 3XL.
Tel. 020 8315 1111
E-mail: enquires@ntrust.org.uk

Ordnance Survey
Romsey Road,
Maybush,
Southampton SO16 4GU.
Tel. 02380 792912
Fax. (Public) 02380 792615
Email: custinfo@ordsvy.gov.uk
Website: www.ordsvy.gov.uk

Ramblers' Association
2nd Floor, Camelford House,
87-90 Albert Embankment,
London
SE1 7TW.
Tel. 020 7339 8500
Fax. 020 7339 8501
Website: www.ramblers.org.uk

Royal Society for the Protection of Birds (RSPB)
The Lodge, Sandy, Beds SG19 2DL.
Tel. 01767 680551
Fax. 01767 692365
Website: www.rspb.org.uk.

Youth Hostels Association
Trevelyan House, Dimple Road, Matlock, Derbyshire DE4 3YH.
Tel. 0870 870 8808
Email: customerservice@yha.org.uk
Website: www.yha.org.uk

Local Organisations
Wales Tourist Board
Brunel House, 2 Fitzalan Road, Cardiff CF24 0UY.
Tel. 029 204 99909
Fax. 029 204 85031
Website: www.visitwales.com

Butterfly Conservation (Wales)
10 Calvert Terrace, Swansea SA1 R5A.
Tel. 01792 642972
Fax. 01792 642985
Email: info@butterfly-conservation.org
Website: www.butterfly-conservation.org

CADW: Welsh National Monuments
National Assembly for Wales

Cathays Park, Cardiff CF10 3NQ.
Tel. 029 2050 0200
Fax. 029 2082 6375
Email: cadw@wales.gsi.gov.uk

Coed Cymru
The Old Sawmill, Tregynon, Newtown, Powys SY16 3PL.
Tel. 01686 650777
Fax. 01686 650696
Email: coedcymru@mid-wales.net
Website: www.coedcymru.mid-wales.net

Council for the Protection of Rural Wales
Ty Gwyn, 31 High Street, Welshpool, Powys SY21 7YD.
Tel. 01938 552525
Fax. 01938 552741
Email: yvcw@aol.com.

Countryside Council for Wales
Maes-y-Ffynnon, Penrhosgarnedd, Bangor, Gwynedd LL57 2DN.
Tel. 01248 385500
Website: www.ccw.gov.uk

Countryside Council for Wales (West area)
Plas Gogerddan, Aberystwyth SY23 3EE.
Tel. 01970 821100.

Glamorgan Heritage Coast Centre
Dunraven Park, Southerndown, Vale of Glamorgan CF32 0RP.

Tel. 01656 880157
Fax. 01656 880931.

Marine Conservation Society
Freepost HR391, Ross-on-Wye
HR9 5BU.
Tel. 01989 566017
Fax. 01989 567815
Website: www.mcsuk.org.

National Trust Office for Wales (South)
Baltic House, Mount Stewart
Square,
Cardiff Bay, Cardiff CF10 5FH.
Tel. 029 204 62281
Fax. 029 204 89103.

Public Transport
Bus Traveline 0870 608 2 608
National Rail Enquires 08457 48
49 50 (www.thetrainline.com)

Ordnance Survey Maps
Explorers
151 (Cardiff & Bridgend)
152 (Newport & Pontypool)
165 (Swansea)
166 (Rhondda & Merthyr Tydfil)

Landrangers
170 (Vale of Glamorgan)
171 (Cardiff & Newport)

Answers to Questions
Walk 1: In the fields above Slade
Wood you will find a number of
hawthorns that have been
drastically affected by the wind.
Walk 2: They are numerous, and a
simple identification book will help
you to recognise small white, large
white, northern brown argus,
clouded yellow, holly blue,
common blue, small heath,
peacock, gatekeeper, small
tortoiseshell, red admiral, painted
lady and dark green fritillary.
Walk 3: The arch will be found
along the main woodland trail.
Walk 4: Fulmars are a rather stiff-
winged seabird that loves to
perform aerial acrobatics in the air
currents that swirl around sea
cliffs. It is not unusual to spot
groups of these all along this walk.
They are rather curious and will
approach quite closely to humans,
but then veer away with a
nonchalant flick of their tail.
Walk 5: 125.
Walk 6: On the western edge of the
walk, near Cogan Plantation, a
fallen tree has been partially carved
to resemble a dragon.
Walk 7: At the foot of the south
door into St Illtud's Church there is
a large fossilised ammonite
embedded in a stone. *Please don't
try to remove it.*
Walk 8: The sundial is on the wall
of St Teilo's Church, dated 1720.
Walk 9: Because the level was
invariably flooded with water, they

used flat-bottomed boats to float the coal out.

Walk 10: There are a number of large wooden sculptures throughout the woodlands of Cwm Carn. The wooden shepherd and his dog stands at Pegwn-y-bwlch.

Walk 11: They are parish boundary letters on a small marker stone beside the triangulation pillar on the summit of Mynydd Twyn-glas.

Walk 12: Common heather and small clumps of cross-leaved heath are found in the early stages of the walk as it climbs above the cwm. The cross-leaved heath has rather more bulbous flowers and its slender leaves are arranged in fours around the stem.

Walk 13: It was the Marchioness of Bute, in 1931.

Walk 14: It was the first camping barn in Wales.

Walk 15: A tree carved into the shape of a buzzard stands just above the campsite above the visitor centre at the end of the walk.

Walk 16: 13 miles to Neath and 16 miles to Pontypridd. The information is contained on a Sustrans Milepost (Route 47), alongside the route.

Walk 17: It is a well.

Walk 18: Just at the entrance to King George V Fields, either side of the stile (and again as you leave through the kissing-gate onto the road) there are commemorative plaques. The one on the right depicts a unicorn.

Walk 19: At two places on the walk, once as it reaches the edge of the moorland, and then again inside the country park boundary, near a watercourse, there are low boundary markers with the letter 'B' surmounted by a stylised crown.

Walk 20: Flat Holm.